The Collector's Anthology
of
Antique Horse Brasses

VOLUME I

First Prize turnout, Wiltshire, England, May Day c.1890

The Collector's Anthology

of

Antique Horse Brasses

✳ ✳ ✳

Richard Bradshaw and Ian Jones

A publication of the National Horse Brass Society
Great Britain

VOLUME I

Copyright © National Horse Brass Society 2011

All rights reserved. No part of this publication may be reproduced, stored in a retrieval system or transmitted, in any form or by any means, electronic, mechanical, photocopying, recording or otherwise, without the prior written permission of the National Horse Brass Society.

***

First published 2011
ISBN 978-0-901100-96-2

***

Printed in Great Britain by
Northend Creative Print Solutions
Clyde Road, Sheffield S8 0TZ

Contents

Introduction 7

Agricultural Brasses 8

Suns, Moons and Stars 13

Horses 18

Bells 23

Early Hanging Brasses 28

Crescents 33

Patterns 36

Ceramics 42

Commemoratives 47

Year Brasses 60

Brewery 62

Trade & Vestry 65

Estate & Armorial 70

Farmer Brasses 72

Saddlers 75

Awards 82

Terrets 94

Oddities 104

Acknowledgements 106

Making it my endeavour first and last,
To serve the present and preserve the past.

—H. S. Richards
Horse Brass Collections, No. 1

Introduction

The National Horse Brass Society was founded in 1975 to encourage and provide a forum for collectors in this unusual field. With publication of the eight-booklet series entitled *Collecting Horse Brasses*, wherein more than two thousand examples of decorative harness brasses are illustrated, the Society achieved what is probably the most comprehensive record yet written on the subject. Offering general information and helpful advice, the series features single and leather-mounted brasses as well as whole collections. Other NHBS publications concentrate on award, saddler, royalty, railway, brewery and bell brasses—all of which have become invaluable for modern collectors. In addition, throughout its 36-year history the Society has printed a biannual Journal about brasses in which members share knowledge and experience.

The existence of such a wide-ranging archive has led many collectors to observe that it might be helpful to have an overview, or summary, of the very finest examples, including both the known and less known, the uncommon and the "one-offs", and those never before published. Most collections hold certain highly cherished examples which have remained in obscurity and are long overdue of permanent record. It is our purpose to begin giving such rarities the recognition they deserve and to present the best of the best, as far as we know to date. Our focus is on brasses we believe meet this standard and, space permitting, we attempt to show them with a maximum of detail. It is also our belief that the selection criteria we have used obviate and make redundant assumed parameters such as rarity factors.

Whether from our own collections or from those scattered about this country and abroad, each example has been imaged on site and individually, in most cases under far less than controlled studio lighting. Photography of horse brasses has always posed a significant technical challenge, so we apologise in advance for aberrations of colour, hue and scale that will be noted.

It is our hope that even experienced collectors will discover in the following pages something new, something exciting, something which perhaps one day may turn up at an antique fair, auction house, or car-boot sale.

R.J. Bradshaw
I.D. Jones

Agricultural Brasses

The plough as an image in early horse brass manufacture was a popular symbol engrained in folklore from the middle ages—as was the phrase "God Speed the Plough", which originated from a 15th Century song, sung during Plough Monday celebrations on the first working Monday after Twelfth Night, when farm labourers returned to the fields following their Christmas holiday. Its usage on horse brasses is therefore one of work association.

[8]

Other, though much rarer symbols include the swingletree device seen in brass No.4. All of the brasses here are early cast types and illustrate this close relationship to work, especially No.6, a splendid example utilised by Ham of Wadebridge to advertise his profession as harness maker.

[9]

Wheatsheaf brasses display another 19th century symbol with roots in ancient folklore. This instantly recognisable trade icon alludes to an entire agricultural production line, from farm crop and harvested grain to the grain merchant, to the miller who ground the flour, to the baker who made the bread, and of course to the brewing industry in the case of barley. The examples shown are mostly early types.

Especially noteworthy, opposite and below, are the pendant brass depicting three separate ears of corn (No.10), the winged-crescent pendant showing the crop as it appears in the field (No.12), and the rare swinger depicting the scythe-wielding labourer who cut the corn (No.15). What the cockerel-on-wheatsheaf represents (No.9) is not known, though as the image appears on an heraldic torse or crest wreath, this may be a brass from a landed estate where the wheatsheaf was one of the oldest charges in heraldry and known as a garb.

Carter brasses also symbolized a trade or profession and were made to appeal to the carters themselves.

This old, though posed image of c.1900, aptly portrays the popular image of the country carter in his felt slouch hat, working smock and whip, a common sight throughout the 19th century and an image that was immortalised in brass.

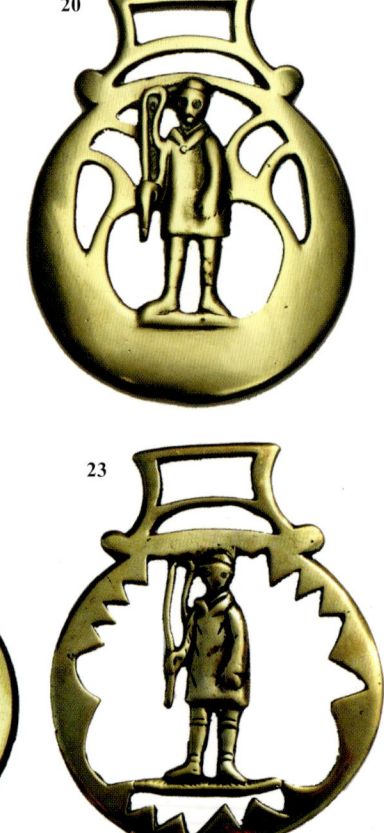

Suns, Moons and Stars

The sun brasses featured opposite are all early examples with an obvious theme—the sunshine that was (and is) so dear not only to agricultural workers but to the British as a nation. Most of these designs can probably trace their origins back to the symbolism of the 18th and 19th centuries, already well known to brass manufacturers. Collectors also prized brasses displaying such ancient devices, attributing unbroken lineage to the harness amulets of early times. It is more likely however that the manufacturers simply copied popular symbols to appeal to working horsemen who, as with the wheatsheaf examples, associated themselves with this imagery. Some of the oldest types may even have been adapted from a previous existence, i.e., similar three-inch, lead-filled sun faces were frequently attached as decorations to embellish Victorian brass bedsteads!

The sun image, known in heraldry as the "sun-in-splendour", was used by several titled families, notably on their carriage harness. The fashion for emulating nobility may therefore have played a part in spreading the use of this device. It also served as a Masonic symbol, was adopted by the old Sun Alliance company, and was commonly employed as a fire insurance plaque.

Brass No. 30 is an early, personalised type made for J. Talbot of Stawley, a farming hamlet near Wellington in Somerset close to the Devonshire border.

No. 32, from the old Sun Flour Mills of St. Leonard Street, Bromley by Bow, London, has a clear trade association and used the existing pattern for No. 33.

Brass No.34 is well-known but has been included because of its age and rare condition. Note also the Victorian registration mark at the one o'clock position, dating this pattern back to 1863.

The large three-inch sun stud (No. 35) conveys a bold solar reference and has the remains of six iron fixing shanks on the back side.

[15]

Common amongst the theories of early collectors, alongside the ones relating to sun brasses, were those with a similar heavenly reference, i.e., examples that relate to star and moon brasses. Once again, most of these were images well known to 19th century heavy horsemen from childhood. The "man-in-the-moon" was a familiar metaphor in folk and fairy tales, as were various star images that became popular trade symbols associated with certain breweries and many public houses.

The stars on these pages are all early cast types with designs simple to manufacture, effective when viewed against a dark leather background and, just as importantly, easy to keep clean!

The double-sided half-moon brasses are amongst the rarest to find nowadays. Early writers often mused that these were of Continental origin, probably Neapolitan, where as in England this symbol had esoteric association with the peasantry. This may well be the case, but whilst researching for this book in Worcestershire with National Horse Brass Society founder Terry Keegan, the original pattern (No.44) for corresponding brass (No. 43) was discovered—so could the latter be another early domestic type or was it a brass manufactured in England for a foreign market?

[16]

[17]

Horses

The symbolism of the horse, either unfettered and free or harnessed for work, needs little explanation. Several of the early cast-intaglio horse designs have a strong resemblance to the chalk hill figures found in England, and we are led to wonder whether these might have inspired brass designers seeking to appeal to heavy horsemen from such areas. Brass No. 49 bears strong resemblance to the most northerly of the chalk figures at Kilburn in Yorkshire, as well as to the one found at Westbury in Wiltshire. The example with raised left foreleg (No. 50) resembles that at Cherhill, whilst the trotting horse (No. 51) is similar to the ones at Hackpen and Broad Town, all found in Wiltshire. The brass inscribed "Star of the West" (No. 57, opposite) is believed to have been worn by a cart horse stallion.

[18]

[19]

60

The strong affinity that working horsemen had with their horses is clear from the names on hameplates and straps, perhaps the most common of which was "Boxer" (No. 62).

61

62

63

64

65

66

[20]

67 68 69

  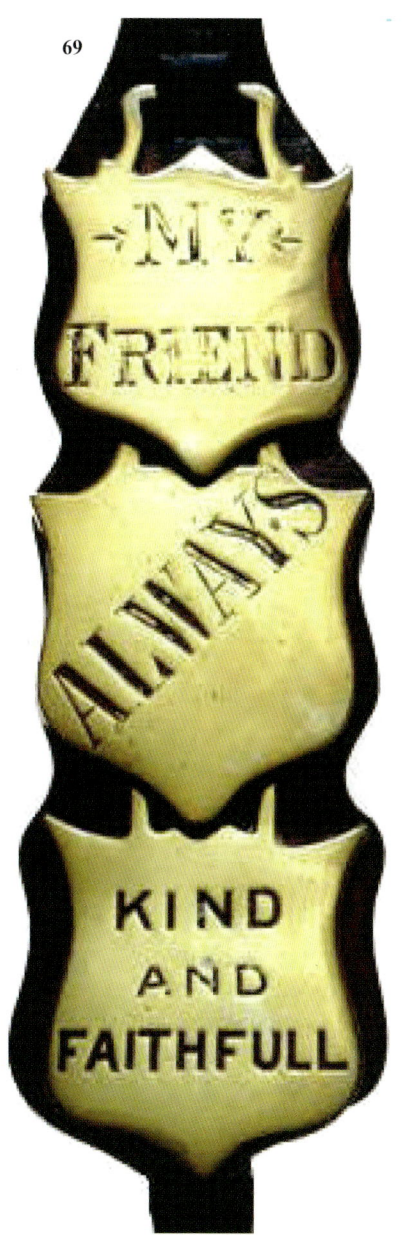

[22]

Bell Brasses

There can be little doubt regarding the popularity of bell brasses with collectors over the years. Most types command a steady price and, as was stated in the 1988 edition of the NHBS publication *Horse Bells*, "Some twenty-five designs of bell face pieces are known from the 19th and early 20th centuries. None can be described as 'common', at least half…are considered to be 'very rare'."

In the intervening years however, three additional designs have been found which are as yet unrecorded. Unusual for bells, No. 75 is not cast but rather an early heavy stamping, with the lugs that hold the bell pin having been sweated on as a second operation. No. 76 is a cast brass which has previously appeared in the literature only as a line drawing. Also a casting, No. 77 with its broad-skirted design, is the sole example ever seen by the authors. Especially rare is No. 78, a casting which for some reason saw only limited production and is actually a variant of its two-bell counterpart (see No. 83).

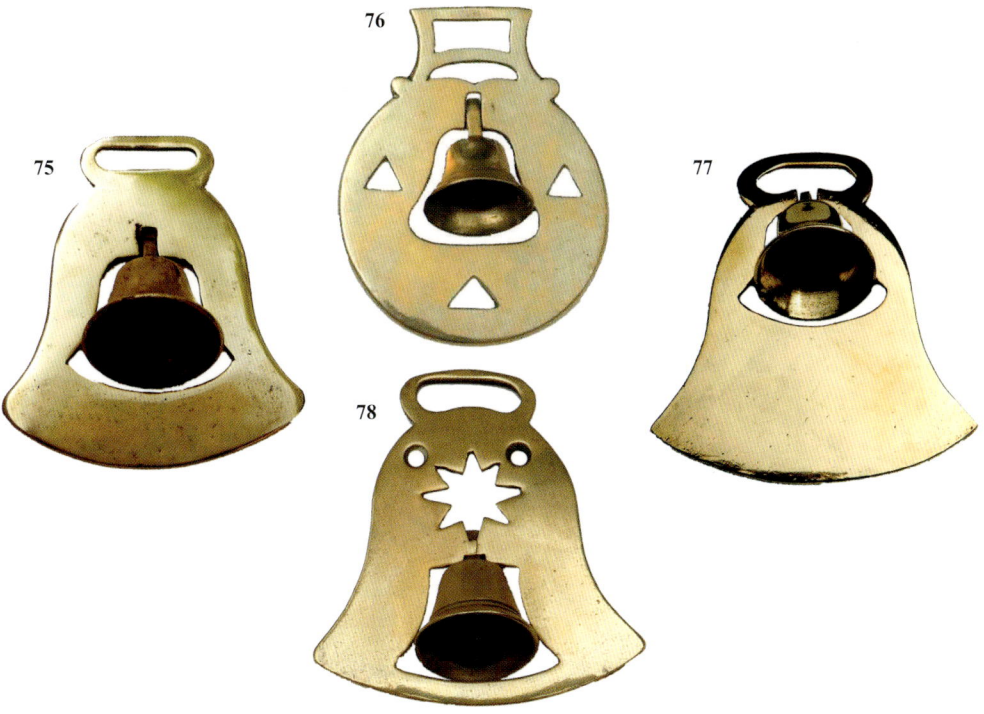

[24]

[25]

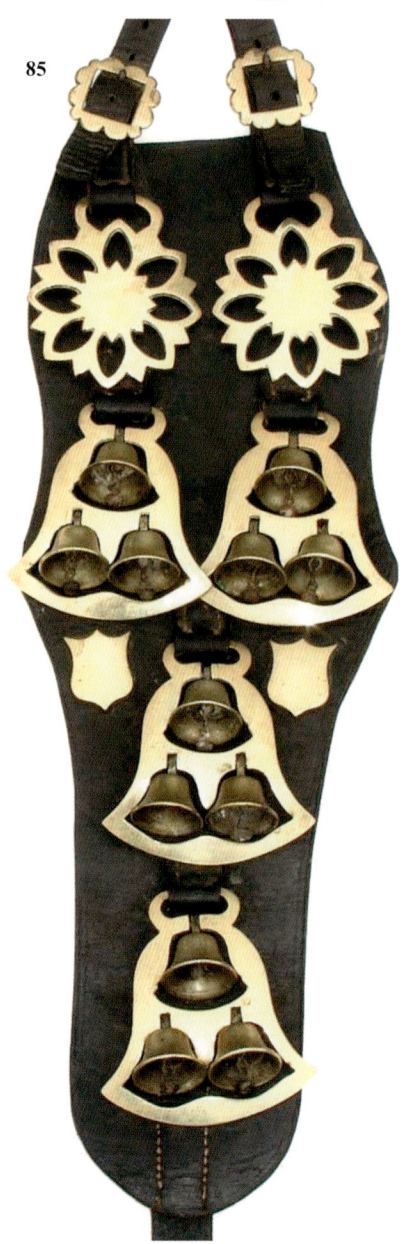

[26]

[27]

Early Hanging Brasses

The earliest brasses often pose the most searching questions, such as when did they first emerge and where? In certain examples we can sometimes find evidence of adaptive practice, i.e. the conversion of earlier stud patterns into brasses that have hangers. No. 88, with the initials "S.M.Y." cast intaglio into the front and displaying both the two casting getts as well as remnants of six iron shanks on the back (No. 89), illustrates this skillful addition of a hanger onto a brass with previous usage. The heart shape engraved "L.B.-Cirencester" (No. 97) and the circular and octagonal sun flashes (Nos. 98 & 96) are similar examples of adaptive practice. The hangers on the boss brasses (Nos. 90-92 & 94) were also separately cast and fastened later, either after previous use on leather or as a second stage during original manufacture.

[28]

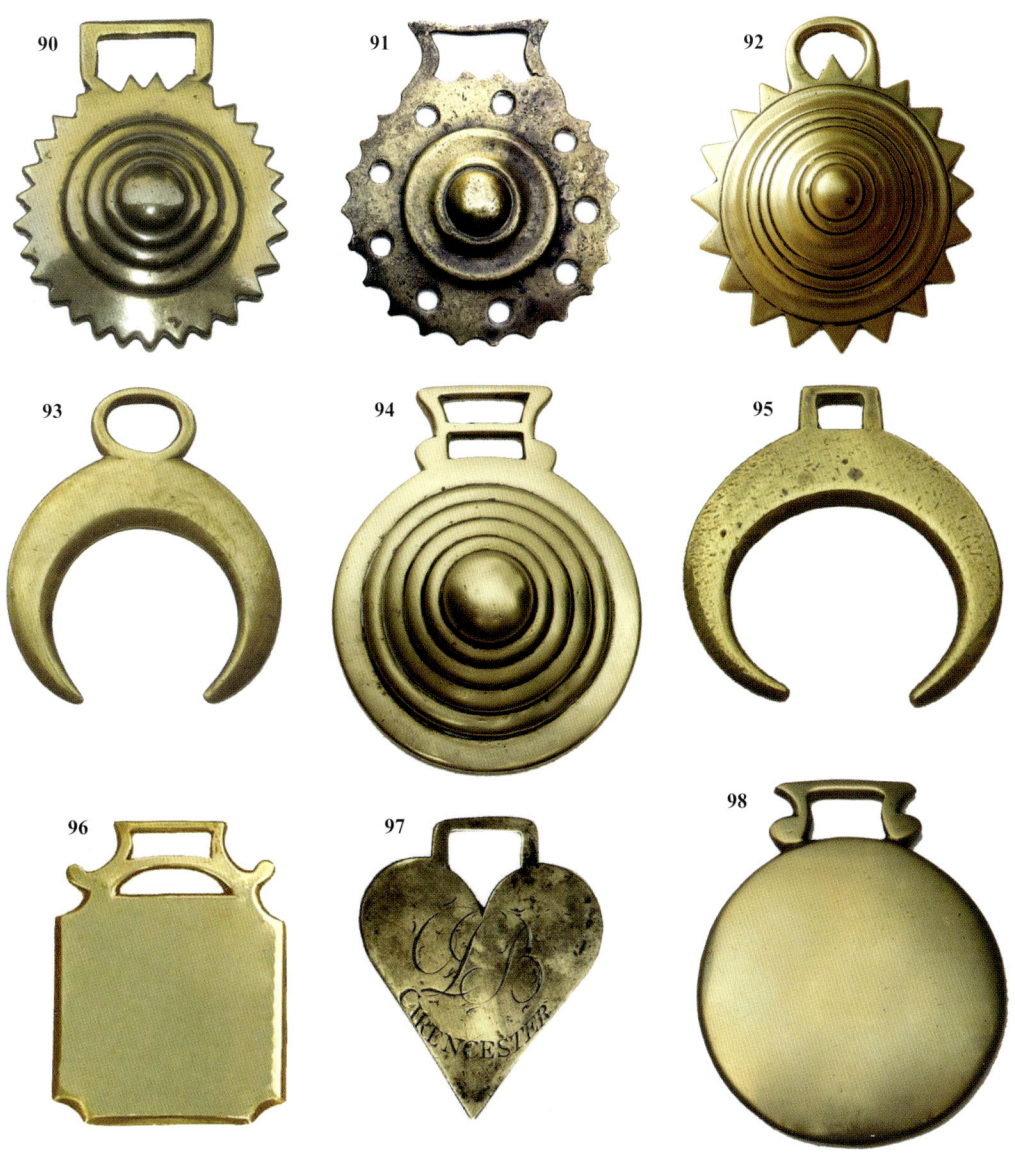

The emerging mode of production is most apparent however, in the types known as Sheffield Stars (Nos. 99-105), many of which were used as patterns for some of the earliest hanging brasses. No other category of harness decoration marks this important stage in the development of horse brass manufacture more clearly.

99

100

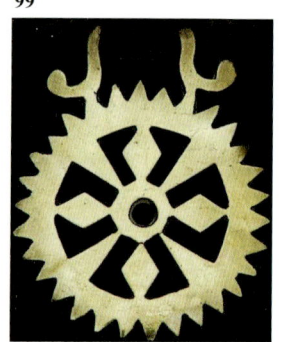

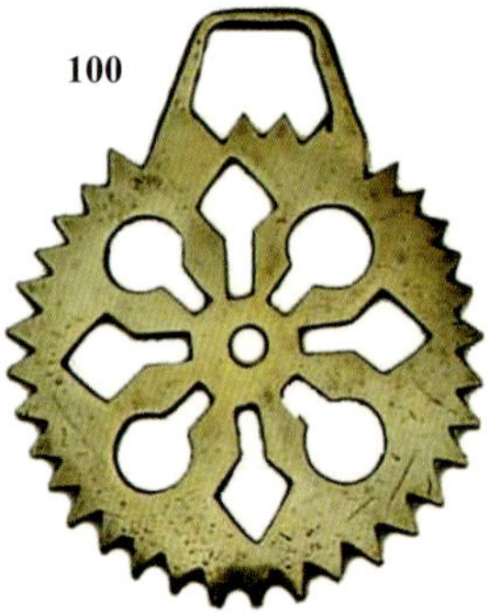

101

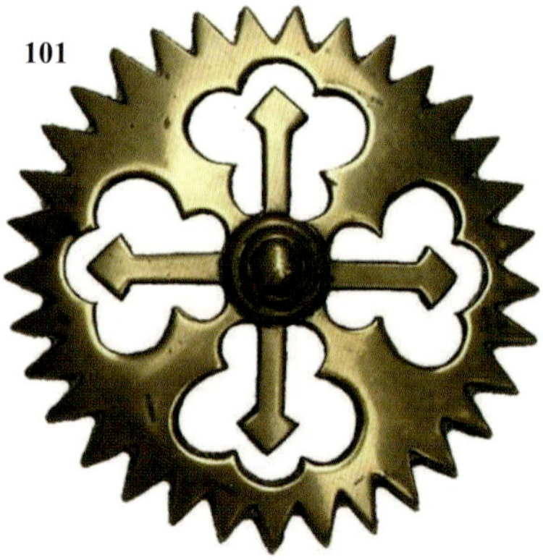

102

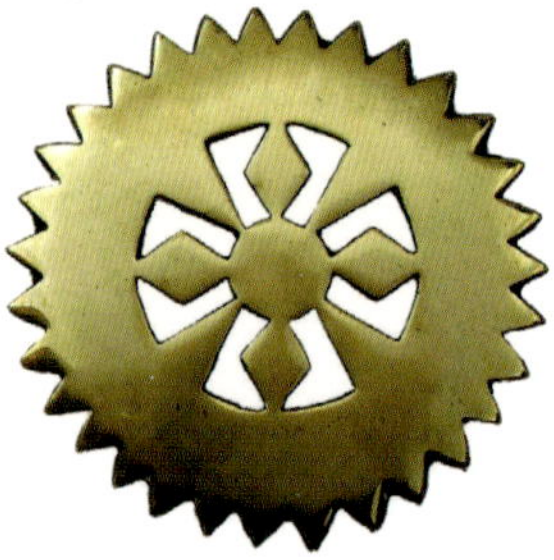

103

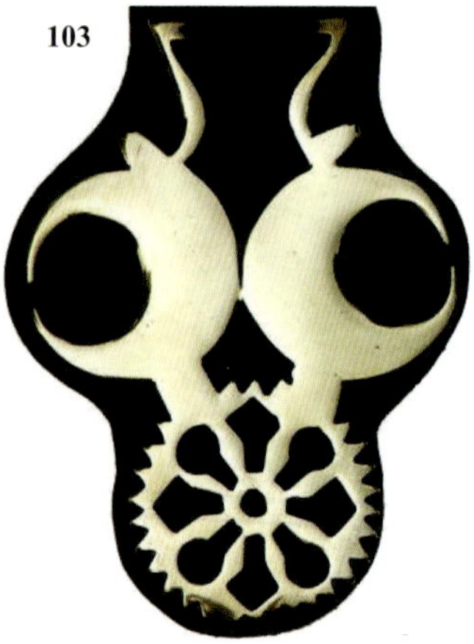

104

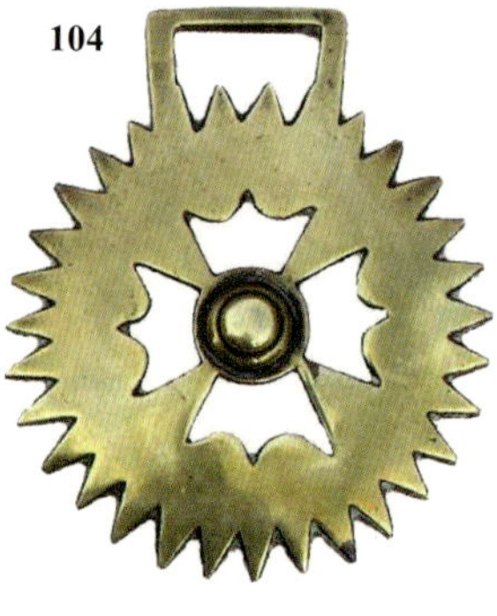

105

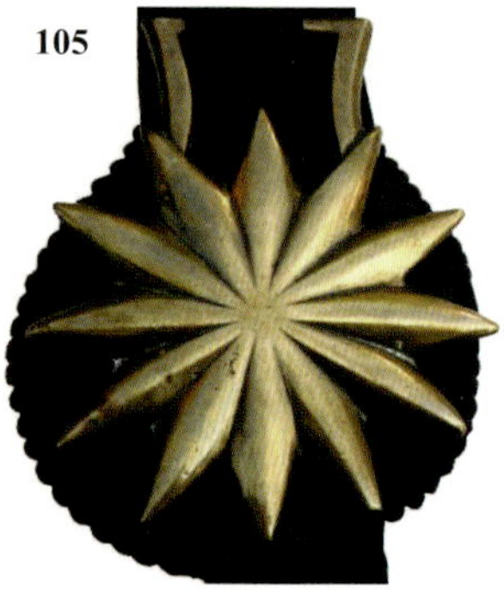

106

107

108

109

The four brasses here all bear a striking similarity, so is this because they were among the very first to be made with integral hangers? Indeed, whenever early-dated or named brasses are found, the odds are that they will be of this pattern or one very similar to it. Unmarked examples are usually reckoned by collectors to date from the late 1850s or early 1860s, and any that bear prior inscribed dates will, until proven otherwise, remain subjects of much debate.

Crescents

The simple crescent form was much used by 19th century brass manufacturers to frame a variety of design motifs. Illustrated below are three examples with a patriotic English Rose theme and three with a geometric petal theme. The detail on Nos. 114 and 115 has survived very well indeed. No. 116 was one of a series illustrated in Thomas Crosbie's catalogue of 1885, and together with No. 117, has a separately cast stud applied later, a sure sign of early age. But is the age of No. 118 consistent with its bold dating?

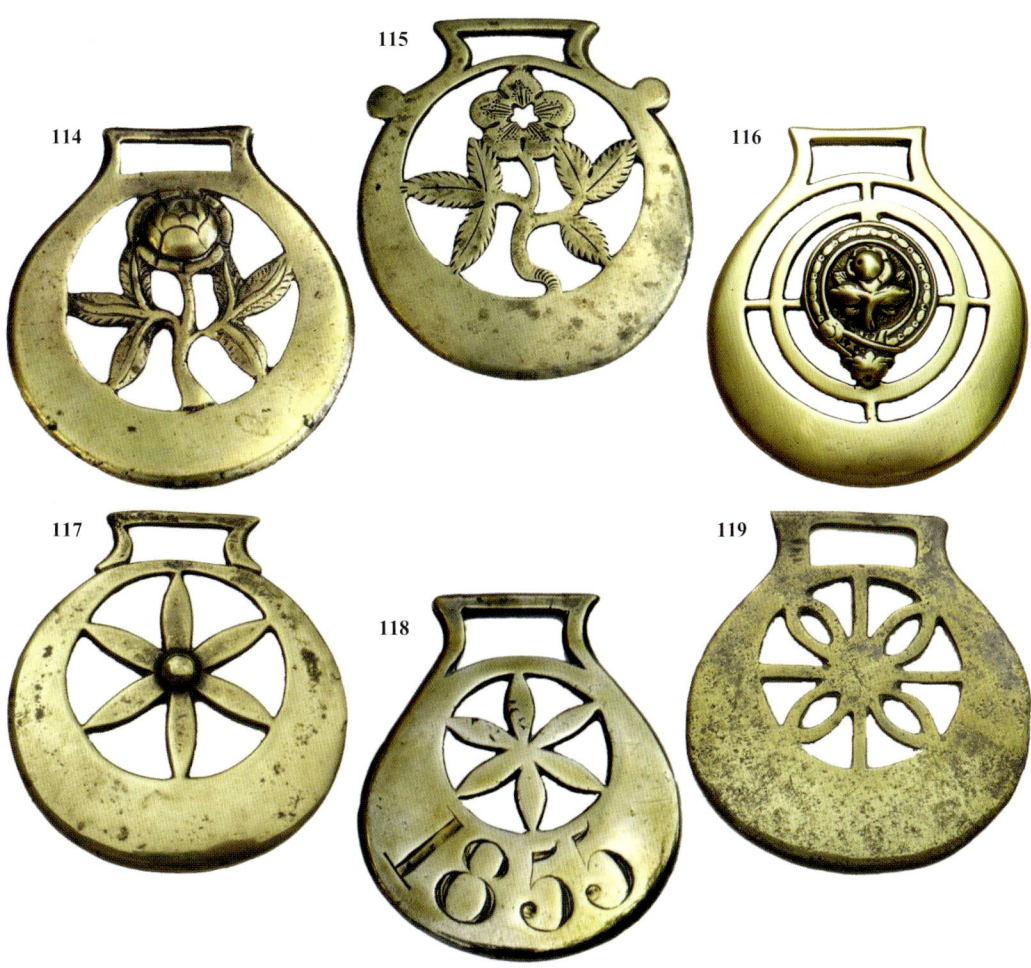

Shown below are three rarely-seen 19th century brasses still on their original leather. No. 120, until now, has not been recorded and No. 121 has a "goal post" hanger, another characteristic of early vintage. Opposite is a selection of early four-inch brasses with crescent-like frames. No. 126 belonged to a family of Derbyshire millwrights c.1870 and has a theme of crossed palm knives (once thought to be saws), serrated for cutting into bales of raw cotton.

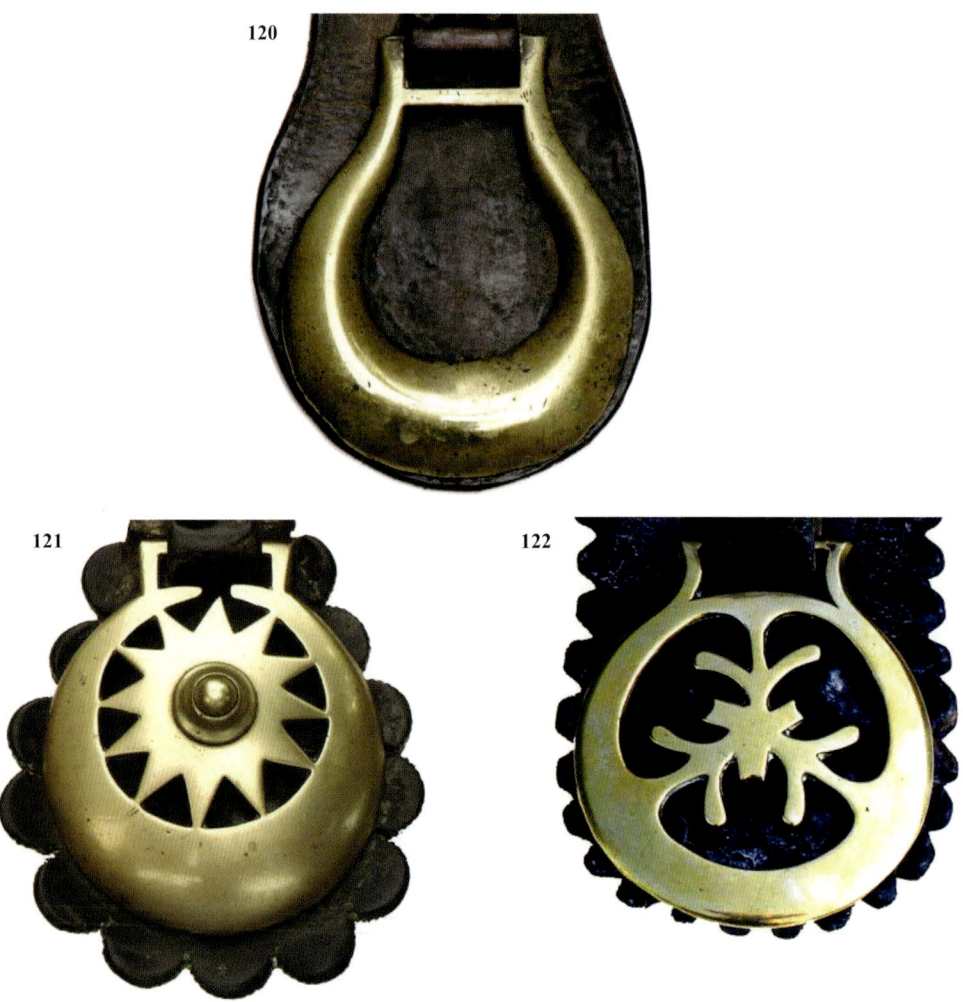

123 124

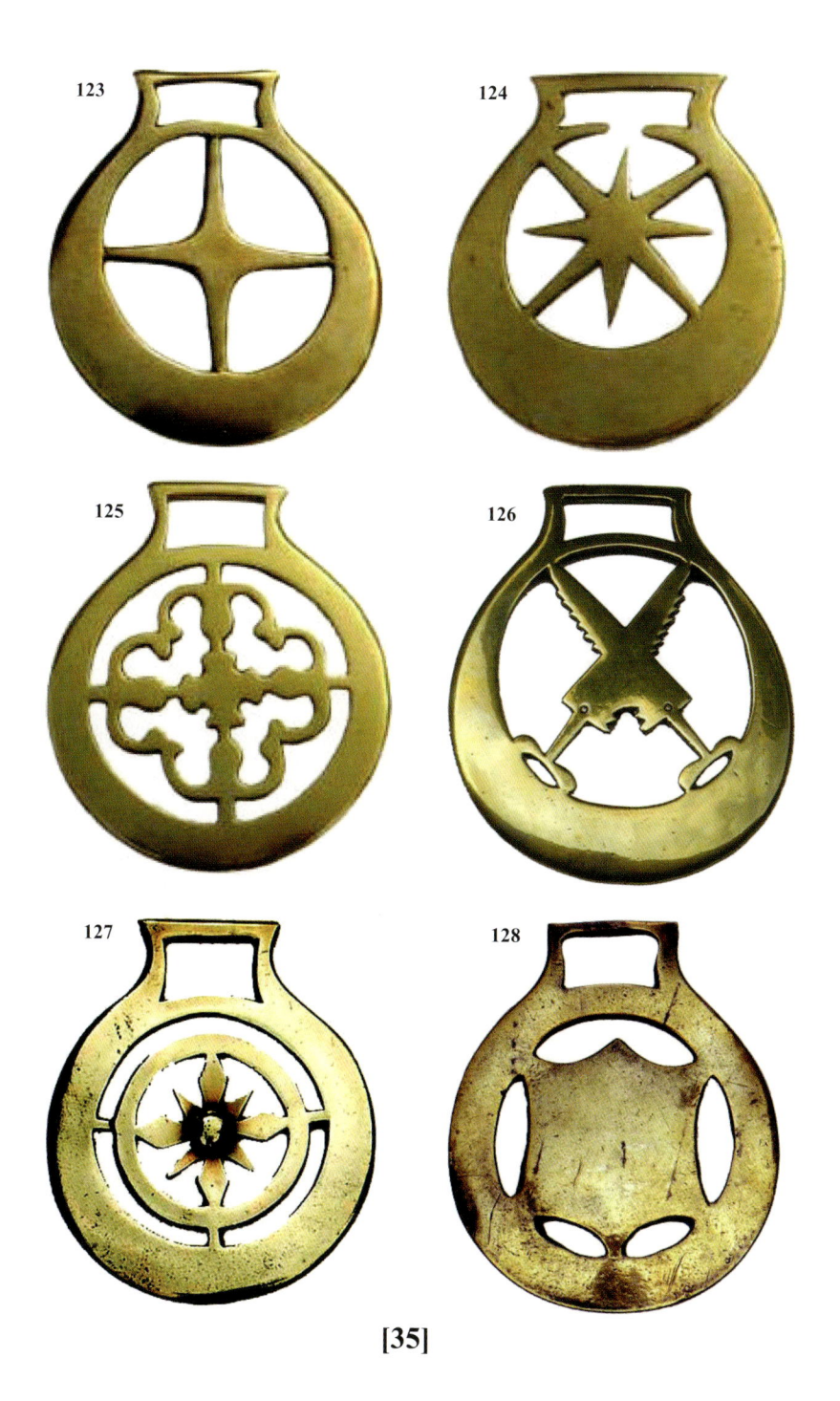

125 126

127 128

[35]

Patterns

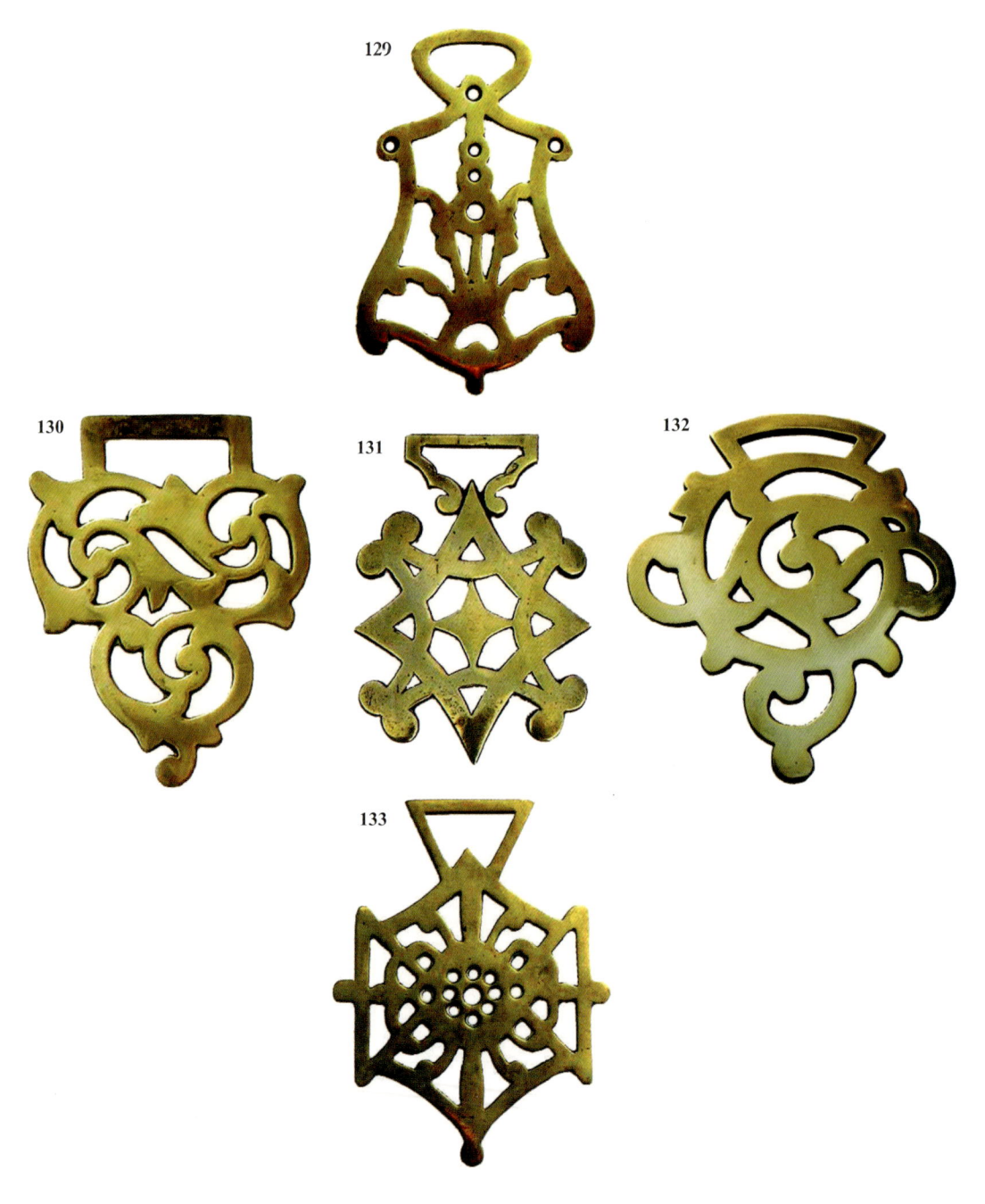

129

130   131   132

133

[36]

134 135

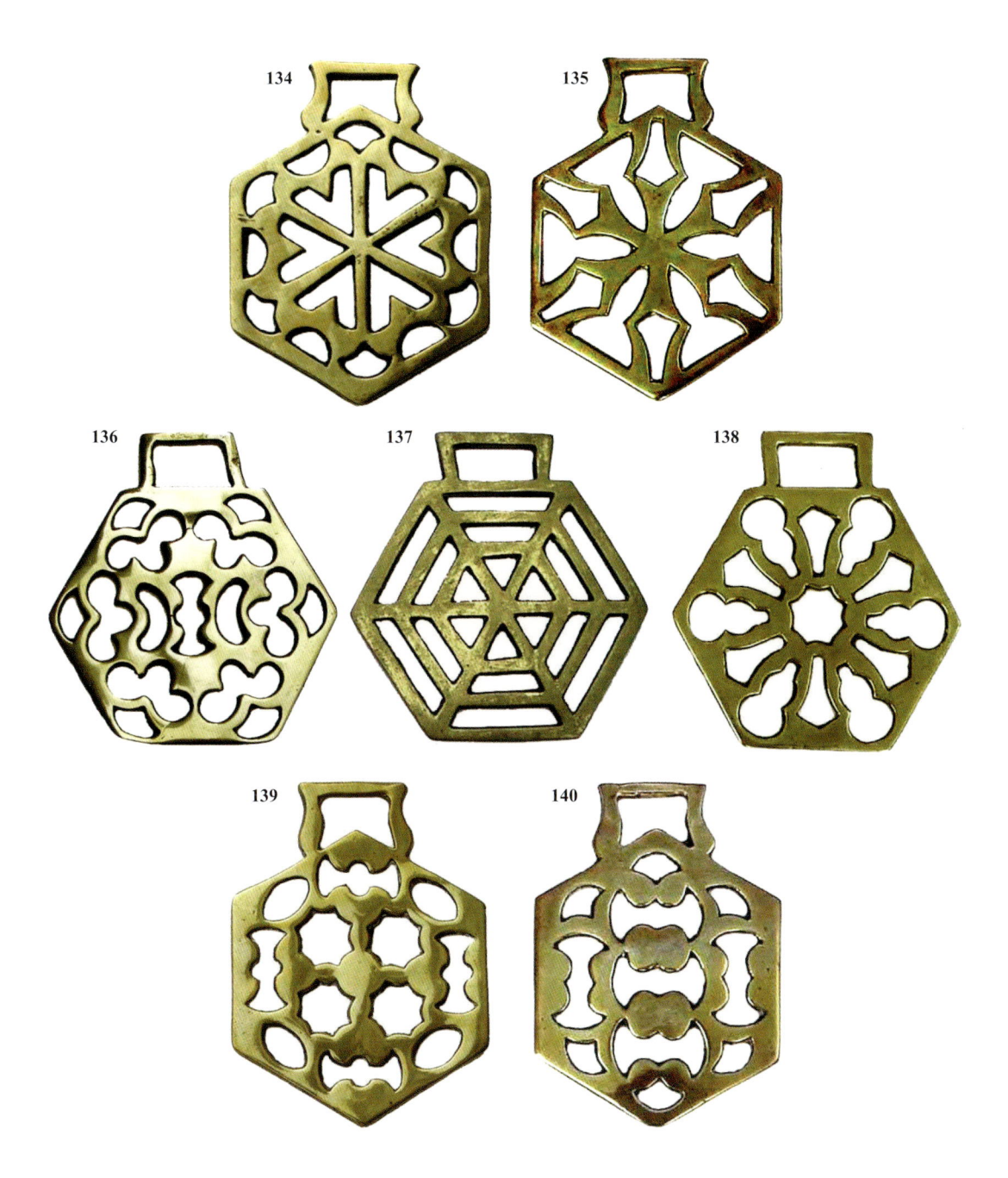

136 137 138

139 140

[37]

The brasses below can only be described as uncommon. Nos. 141 and 143 are later examples, probably dating from the 1890s or early 1900s. Pattern No. 142 might seem to be an early art deco design, whilst No. 145 incorporates a more traditional horseshoe motif.

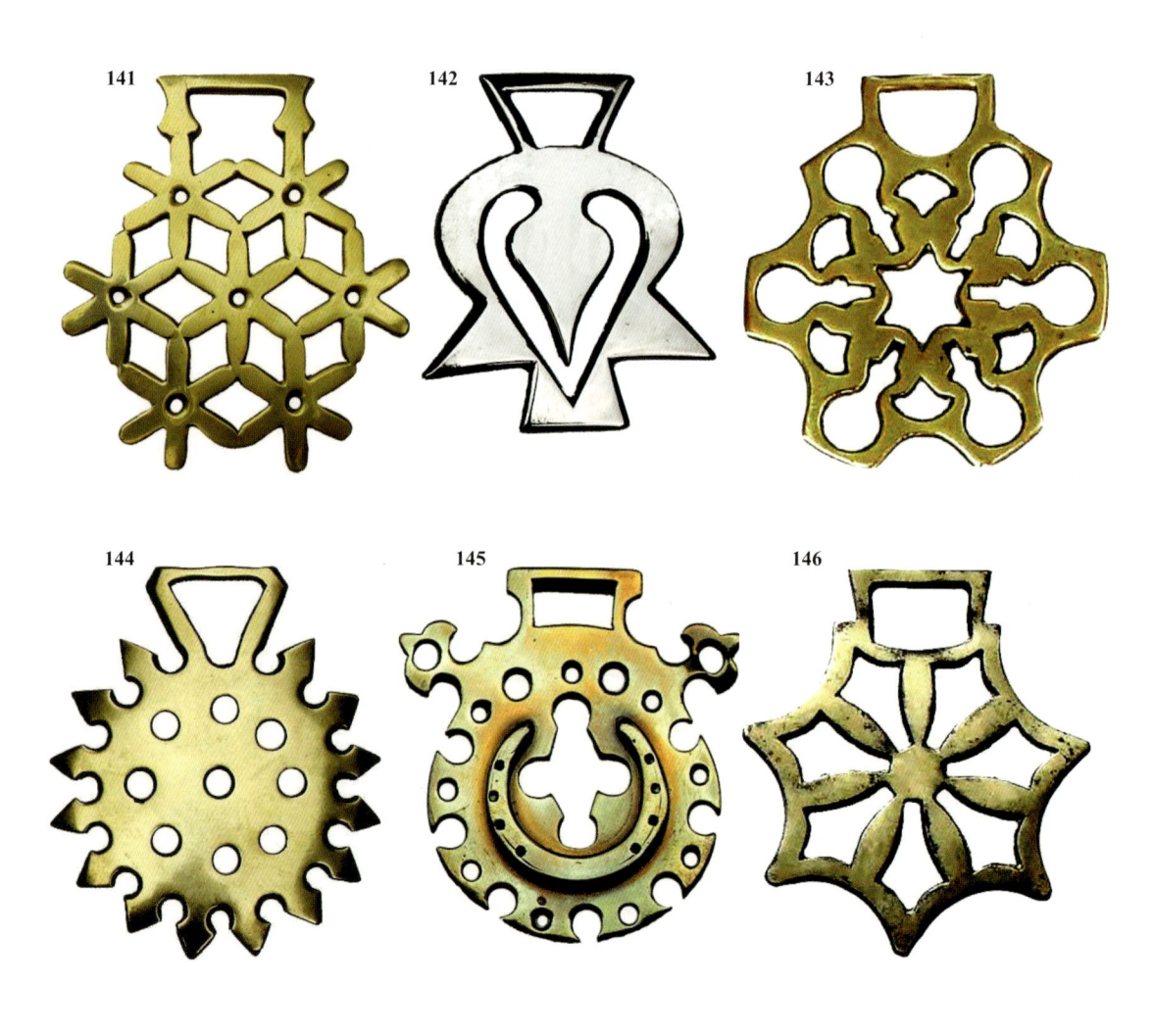

141

142

143

144

145

146

[38]

Increased detail on a brass meant increased surface area that needed hand-finishing. Many pattern brasses are evidence of highly skilled craftsmanship and a proud work ethic that eventually gave way to mass production, which certainly accounts for the rarity of the examples illustrated here. What the bird and leaf represent (No. 147) is not known. No. 148 is a pattern that has seldom survived intact due to its delicate design. No. 150 is shown on its original red cloth backing.

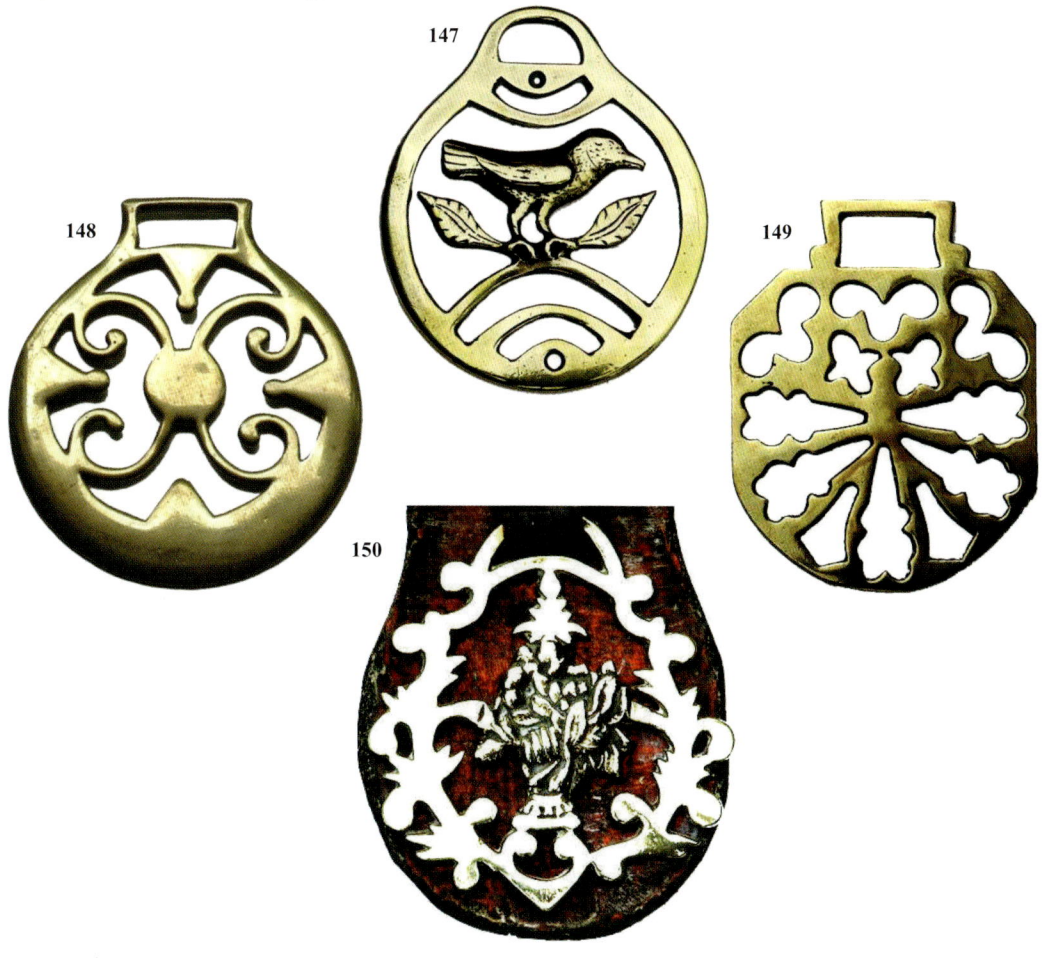

Nos, 151-155 below are four-inch brasses of great age, possibly dating from the 1860s or 1870s. The passage of time has made it difficult to trace regional origin, but No. 153 was first owned by a Lancashire chemical manufacturer in Accrington, so does the unusual design relate to a laboratory beaker?

The examples shown opposite are also early types. Nos. 156 and 157 were cast by the same manufacturer. No. 158 is a splendid cross-moline pattern which has the remains of two 8mm casting getts on the reverse. No. 159 would clearly have required much hand-finishing. No. 160 has an applied central boss and dates earlier than No. 161, where the boss was cast integrally.

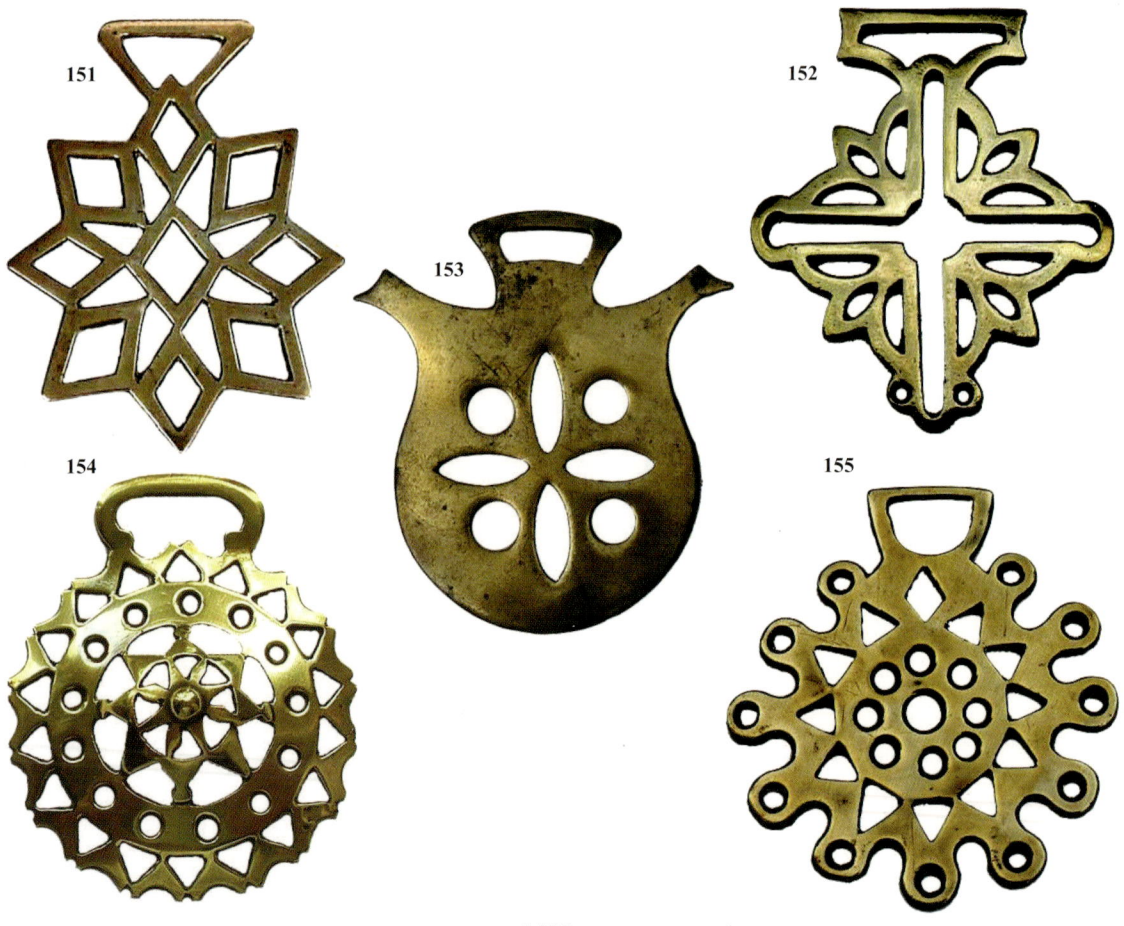

[40]

156 157

158 159

160 161

Ceramics

162

163

164

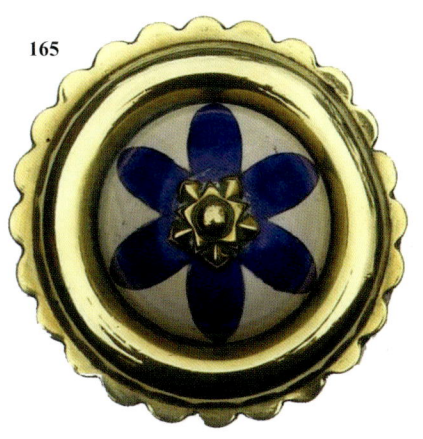

165

166

167

[44]

168

[45]

169   170   171

[46]

Commemoratives

During their many trips and photographic sessions for this volume the authors were amazed to discover the many royalty commemorative brasses that have passed down either unrecorded or with scant visibility. Was this perhaps because smaller, localised foundries produced only limited quantities that never achieved widespread circulation?

The three examples below are all quite thinly cast. Nos. 172 and 173 have finely beveled edges on the reverse and small, very similar getts. Does this suggest that these brasses came from the same foundry? The voided cross of No. 173 is possibly based on a north Irish version of the Celtic cross, so was this design intended to appeal to the heavy horsemen of a certain region?

172

173

174

[47]

No. 175 is a two-part hybrid of both cast and stamped sections and stands alone as one of the finest Victorian commemoratives ever produced. The central bust is a stamping, common to several other rare brasses, and is sweated onto three protruding shoulders along the inside edge of the cast frame. Nos. 176 and 177 show freestanding busts cast integrally. The detail that has survived on all three examples is nothing short of fantastic. This is probably because they saw only event-specific use and were then stored away, or were purchased simply as souvenirs and never placed on harness. Commemorative brasses in many collections display such excellence of detail.

Below are other hybrid examples that combine a stamped central bust or crown with a cast base or frame. The bust on Maltese cross type No. 179 is identical to the one on No. 175 but has clearly seen much polishing and use on harness. The applied crown on No. 178 is also a stamping. Brass No. 180 illustrates the use of such crowns with yet another frame, this one possibly resulting from a surplus left with Birmingham manufacturers after a series of post-1881 changes in military headgear. The example here did in fact bear strong resemblance to the new helmet plates of that era.

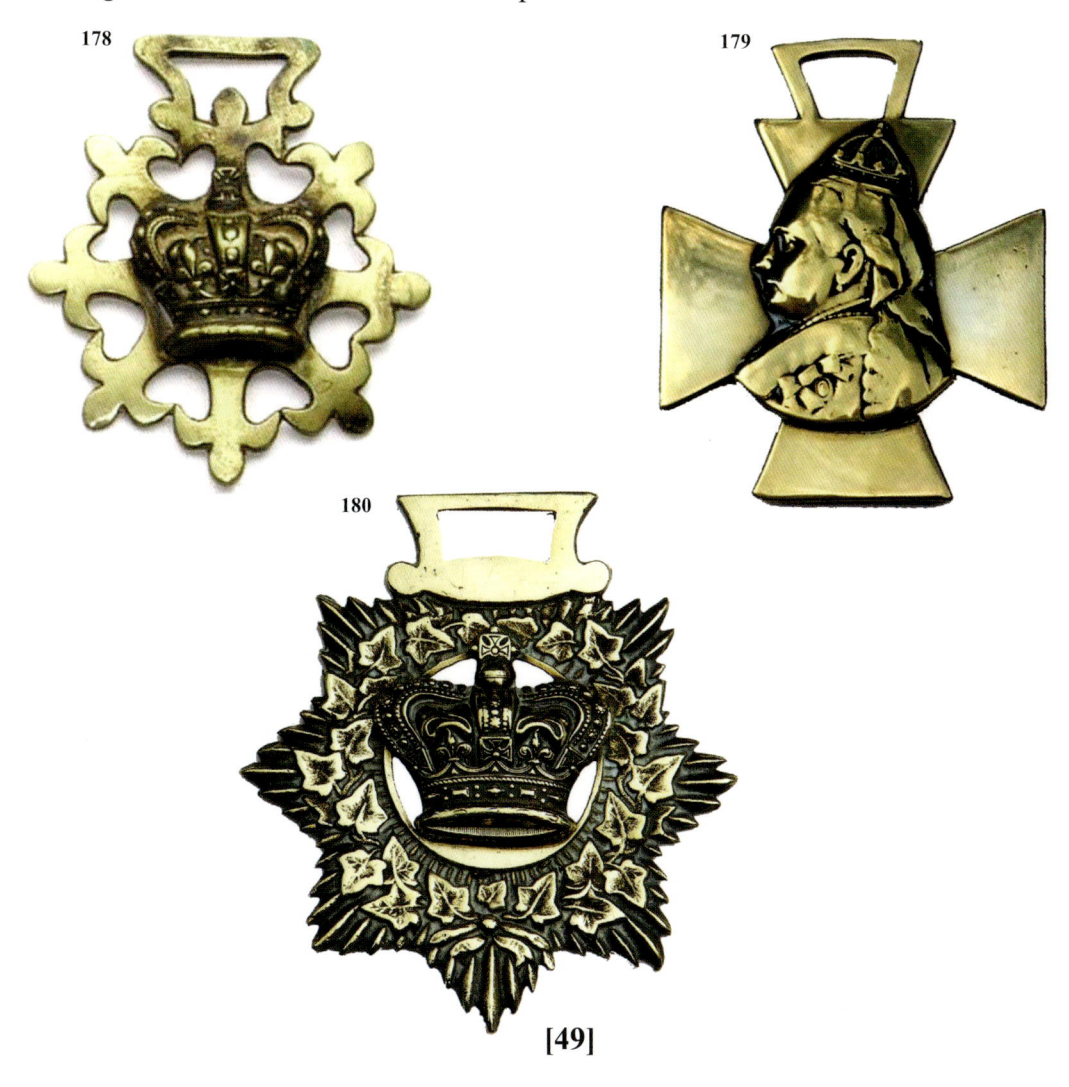

181

182 183

184

[50]

The crown and the royal bust were highly effective commemorative symbols. The crowns on Nos. 185 and 186 incorporate lead-filled brass stampings which, all too often, were effaced over time by normal polishing and wear. Fortunately this father-and-son pair, clearly from the same manufacturer, survived. The busts on stamped brasses Nos. 187 and 188 were pressed into the blanks as a second step, but by omitting the usual voids on either side of the figure, two fairly common brasses became very rare specimens.

Perhaps the best method of displaying royalty brasses, especially in multiples, is on their original leather as part of the decorated harness. Here and on the next pages are undisturbed original martingales that require few words. Examples Nos. 191 and 192, opposite, commemorate both the new King in 1902 and the great affection felt by the British people for their late Queen.

191 192

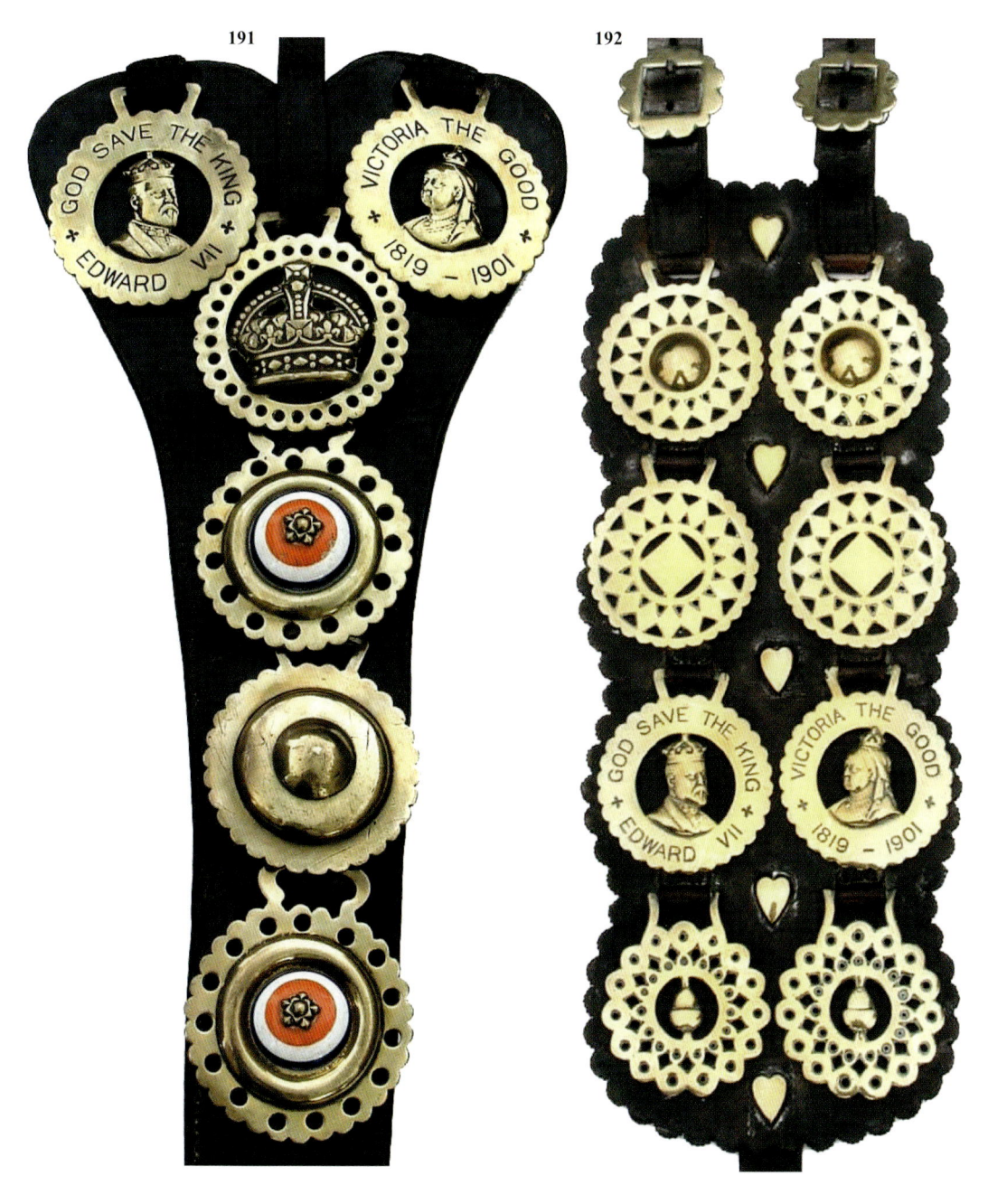

[53]

No. 193 displays everything of importance to its owner—his farm (the wheatsheaves), his horses, his Queen, her heir (the Prince of Wales feathers)—all proudly heralded by the jingle of a bell when worn! How could any martingale speak with greater eloquence?

[54]

Example No. 195 is a collector's dream. Using a nice balance of rare photographic and ceramic brasses, this martingale was created especially to celebrate the 1911 Coronation. Uncommon here is the survival of the photographic centres, which are frequently missing or in very poor condition.

195

Example No. 196 shows how multiple crowns on this 1902 set of harness were used to create a strong visual impression. Did omission of the date and other identifying detail offer the possibility of continued use? Nos. 197 and 198, opposite, are a wonderful pair of martingales that commemorate both Victorian jubilees. They once belonged to H. S. Richards.

196

197

198

[57]

For the above 1902 hame plate, No. 199, three bell terrets were cleverly secured between two pieces of stitched leather to produce a stunning effect. Nos. 200-202, opposite, are original rosettes that illustrate the liberal use of colour to accent harness decorations. Whenever we look at black and white photographs of the early 1900s, these vivid icons of the period serve to brighten our recall. Rosette pairs such as the two matched examples shown are rarely found together nowadays.

[58]

200

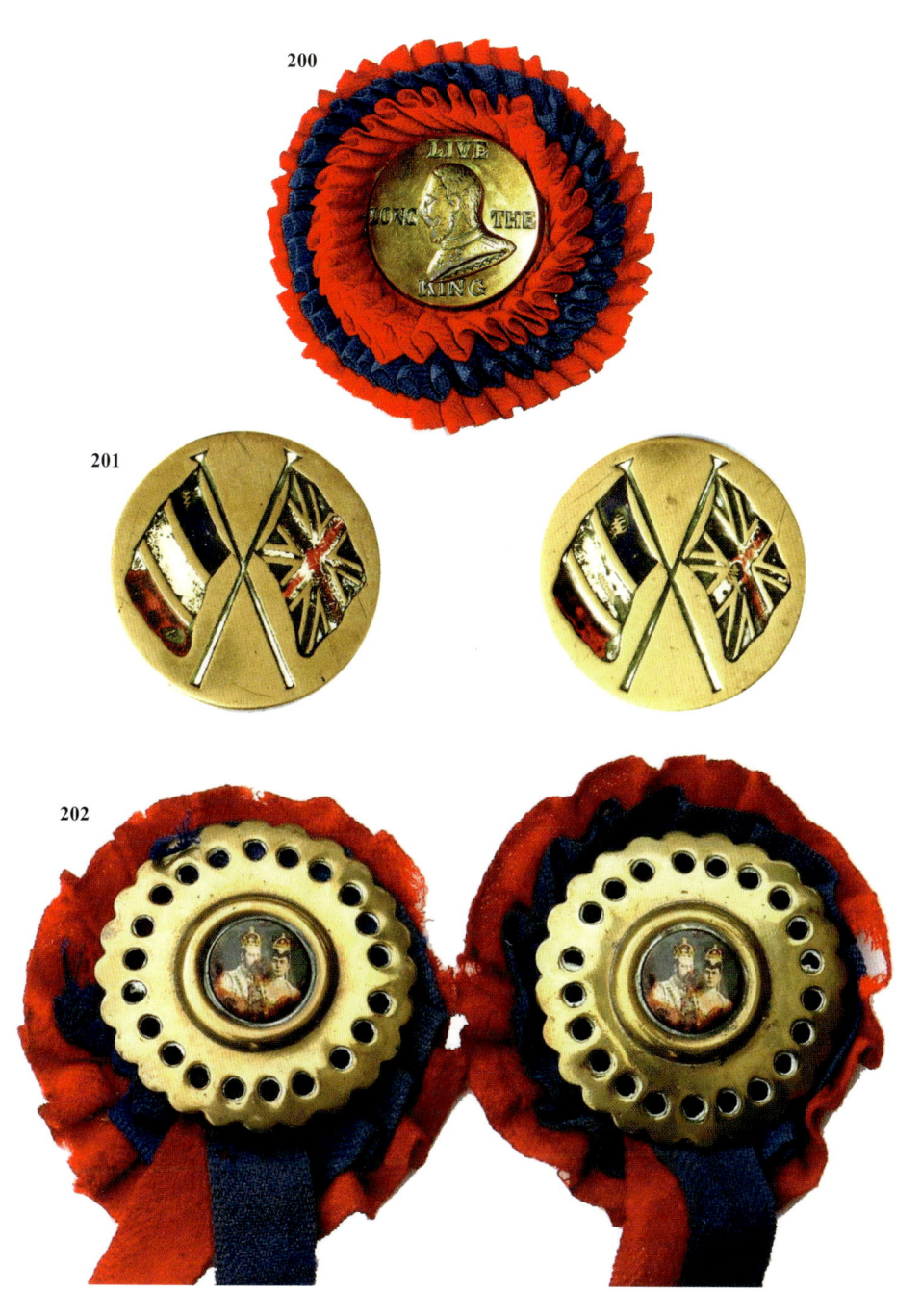

201

202

Year Brasses

Associated closely with Victorian commemoratives were brasses dated with a specific year, especially those bearing the Queen's crown and cipher. Nos. 207 and 208, opposite, were produced by the same manufacturer and likely cast from the same lead pattern. The three V.R. brasses, Nos. 204-206, also came from a single foundry, but note the slight change in rendering the hanger between each of these examples.

Because the indicated dates do not always relate to royal celebrations, these types create endless debate as to how and why they were used, and whether they are in fact as old as they might seem. Except for No. 206, which clearly was produced for the 1897 Diamond Jubilee, all the brasses here leave unanswered questions. Could they simply have been awards given at local parades in smaller venues? Or do they commemorate the start-up of a business, a birth, an anniversary or some other kind of personal event? And is the year indicated by the brass consistent with its date of manufacture? Indeed, for many collectors the ambiguities raised by such year brasses are inextricably linked with the overall fascination of the hobby.

203

[61]

Brewery

Collecting brewery harness brasses is a specialty unto itself known as "breweriana", with an appeal stretching across a broad diversity of antique enthusiasts. In many cases such brasses are all that remain of local breweries that started in the 18th and 19th centuries but were later absorbed into much larger companies. Massey's Burnley Brewery (No. 209) was founded in 1750 and taken over by Charrington United Breweries of London in 1966. The Black Country brewery J&J Yardley of Bloxwich (No. 210) was merged into The Old Wolverhampton Breweries of London in 1910. An attractive oval design was employed by the Coombe Valley Brewery of Wotton-under-Edge for their brass (No. 211). Example No. 212 has no specific provenance but, with both ends of the barrel visible, is a well-worn adaptation of a rare 19th century stud pattern.

[62]

Terret No. 213 announced the Northampton Brewery Company, so renamed by the Phillips brothers in 1873 and continuing until 1960, when it was purchased by brewing giant Watney Mann of London. The white brass tumbler (No. 214) comes from the old Inniskilling Brewery of County Fermanagh in Ireland. The barrel terret (No. 215) is a more generic brewery type, though set here in a rare winged frame. The white brass stud (No. 216) belonged to Sydney Evershed, the brewer and MP for Burton-on-Trent, whose brewery was merged after his death in 1909 to become part of Marston, Thompson & Evershed. Stud No. 217 once decorated a harness used c.1899-1906 by Thomas William Elvy's Dursley Steam Brewery in Gloucestershire.

In 1886 The Leamington Brewery advertised using a bold, nearly twelve-inch brass hameplate, No. 218. This Warwickshire company, owned by Messrs. Lucas, Blackwell & Arkwright, had already been in business for 47 years, but other such dated harness decorations are not known. Example No. 219 is an equally large brewery hameplate of shaped leather. The barrel studs flank a magnificent sun motif of three rotating discs, fixed by a threaded centre boss.

218

219

Trade & Vestry

Throughout the 19th and early 20th centuries most of the short haulage in towns and cities was done by working horses, creating a large demand for trade and vestry brasses. The examples below are from the thriving Liverpool area, where many hundreds of haulage and other companies, large and small, serviced the busy dockyards and booming economy. No. 221 belonged to William Harper, a well known Liverpool haulage company. No. 223 identified boat-builder Joseph Harry Taylor, whose yard was located near Tower Wharf in Chester on the Shropshire Union Canal. No. 224 advertised Garlick, Burrell & Edwards, a removals business operating from Bootle, and No. 225 was from the Leeds & Liverpool Canal Company.

Nos. 226, 227 and 229 are corn merchant and miller's brasses. The shield stud from Bath is an early type, and the freestanding sack is an especially nice example. No. 230 belonged to John Hitchens, a forage contractor and corn merchant from Plymouth.

[66]

No. 232 is of white brass, wonderful in its bold simplicity, though just where and in what context it was used are not known. Vestry brass No. 235 displays the Newcastle-upon-Tyne coat of arms, and No. 236 was issued by the Ramsbottom Urban District Council in Yorkshire. Still a mystery is No. 237, where the pyramid trademark and company have yet to be identified.

Vestry example No. 238 below is a matched set from the City of London Corporation. No. 239 is from the City of Nottingham, where the corporation stables near the cattle market were still being used well into the 1950s.

238

239

No. 240 is a distinctive trade example that once belonged to R&W Paul, maltsters and animal feed producers of Kings Lynn and Grantham. No. 241 identified Thomas Moy, an Essex coal merchant acquired in 1929 by Rickett, Smith & Co. Limited of East London. Research to date has failed to confirm Nos. 242 and 243, though Dyke may have referred to a Midlands foundry.

Estate & Armorial

Estate brasses were produced to order and in limited quantity. Because of their non-specific designs, establishing positive identification can represent a challenge. No. 244 belonged to Henry Leonard Campbell Brassey (1870-1958), 1st Baron Brassey of Apethorpe in Northamptonshire, a dedicated horseman and a cavalry officer in the Great War. No. 245 clearly comes from the Pembroke family estates at Wilton in Wiltshire and was engraved to commemorate the 1861 succession to title and lands by George Robert Charles Herbert, 2nd Baron of Lea and subsequently 13th Earl of Pembroke, following the death of his famous father Lord Sidney Herbert, 1st Baron of Lea, who had served as Secretary at War during the Crimean conflict. The provenance for Nos. 246 and 247 remains obscure, though in fact the crown pearls respectively suggest the crests of viscount and baron.

[70]

Armorial or heraldic brasses originated on the carriages of titled families and the harness of their heavy horses. Such decorations soon came to be seen as fashionable amongst ordinary working horsemen, creating a demand for similar designs which the brass manufacturers were only too happy to exploit. Birds and beasts featured prominently on these armorial types. In the Leeds and Sheffield areas the phoenix and the owl were especially popular. More national in appeal were the griffin-like dragon for Wales and the lion for England and Scotland. Of all the lions that appeared on horse brasses in various forms, the most unusual was example No. 252, the lion facing or "loggerhead", a design first appearing in Matthew Harvey's 1880 catalogue.

Farmer Brasses

Amongst the most valuable and sought-after brasses are those bearing a name, a farm, a date, or perhaps a regional location. Such examples were often central to magnificent displays of decorated harness at county fairs, horse shows, parades and other special events and served to identify the proud owners of the turnouts. The examples shown below and opposite, all early cast types, illustrate this practice: Thomas Wheeler from Winstone near Cirencester, 1847 (No. 254); Frederick Henry Ford Tabor of Burdensball Farm near Wilton, 1869 (No. 255); Samuel Tysoe, Esquire, of Rumer Hall Farm near Welford-on-Avon, 1878 (No. 256); and Richard South of Mitchell Farm in Eastnor near Ledbury, 1878 (No. 257).

In 1894 James Farmer Parker started at Little Frome Farm in Bromyard (No. 258), but had a second brass cast in 1904 when he moved to another location (No. 260). Edward Heward farmed at Ridgeway Farm in Nunney near Frome (No. 259). As for the brasses of Samuel Humphries 1850 (No. 261), J. Amor of Avon Farm (No. 262) and Edmund Bloodworth 1862 (No. 263), more specific provenance awaits further research.

John Thomas White (No. 264) farmed at Pool Farm in Corsley near Warminster between 1890 and 1915. George Keel of Corston near Malmesbury, whose brass (No. 265) is dated 1906, owned Wheatsheaf Farm and the neighboring Wheatsheaf pub, both of which still exist. H.E. Bourne (No. 266) was farming at Erlestoke near Devizes in 1911. In Warminster E.J. Parrott of Bugley Farm (No. 267) and George Hill (No. 268) both had personalised brasses made in 1925, but were they friends or rivals?

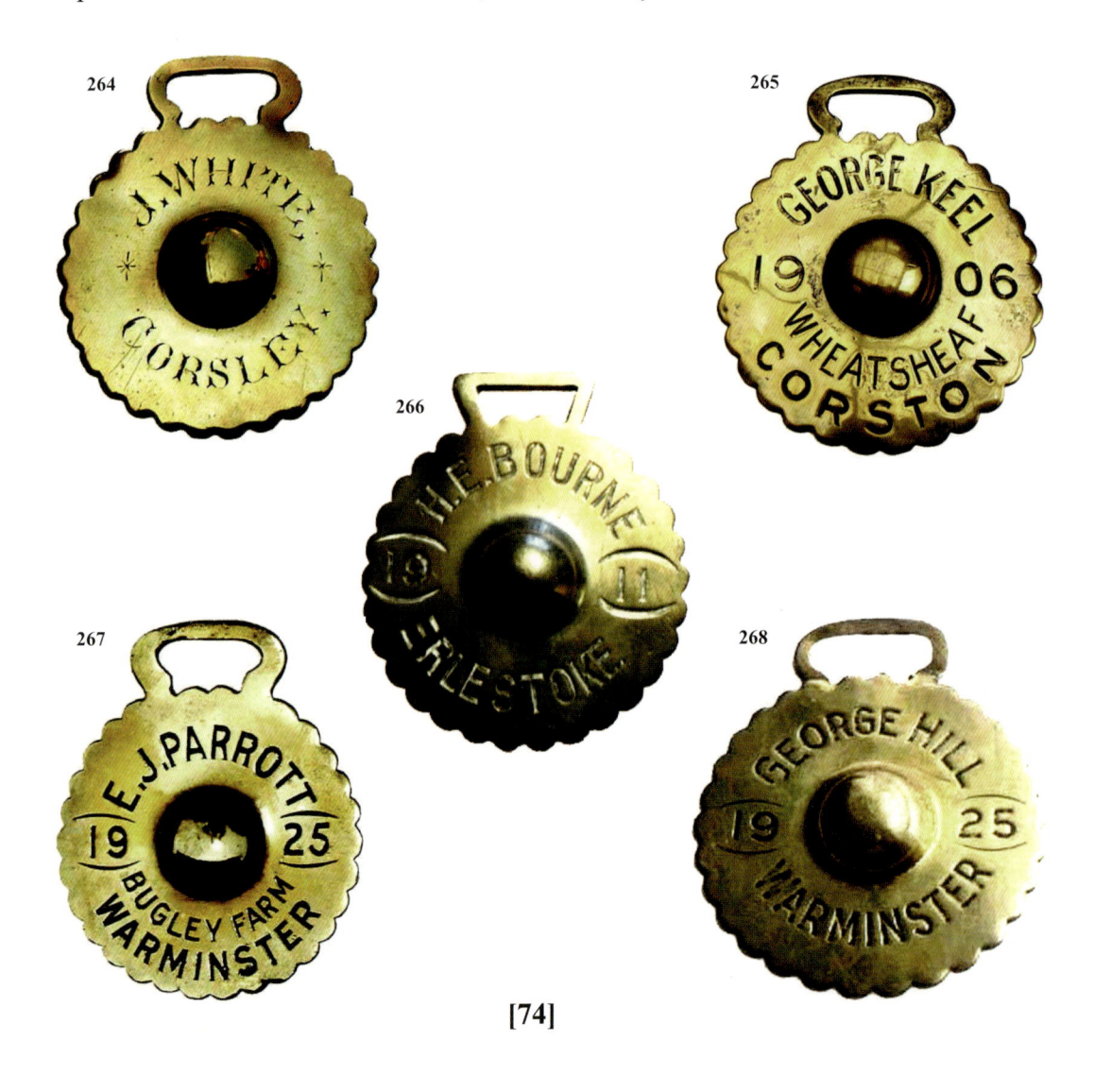

264

265

266

267

268

Saddlers

By the time the heavy horse era was reaching its peak at the end of the 19th century, there were thousands of skilled craftsmen throughout the realm who made their living as saddlers and harness makers. Just as the products of today bear the manufacturer's trademark, the harness of that period was branded by a distinctive horse brass bearing the maker's name. Such brasses are now highly prized by collectors. The few we have selected for inclusion in this volume may be seen as representative examples, but no attempt is made to detail their complete provenance. Each brass conceals its own history, and the research involved in bringing this story to light offers a task at once fascinating and challenging. Our aim here is merely to identify.

No. 269: Williams & Son of Kings Street and 10-11 Lammas Street in Caermarthen were in business from 1871 until 1885 and possibly later.

No. 270: Henry Green is recorded on Gilbert Street in Haslingden from 1871 to1880. By 1903 the business had moved to Manchester Road, from where the family continued a lengthy association with the harness trade up to 1940.

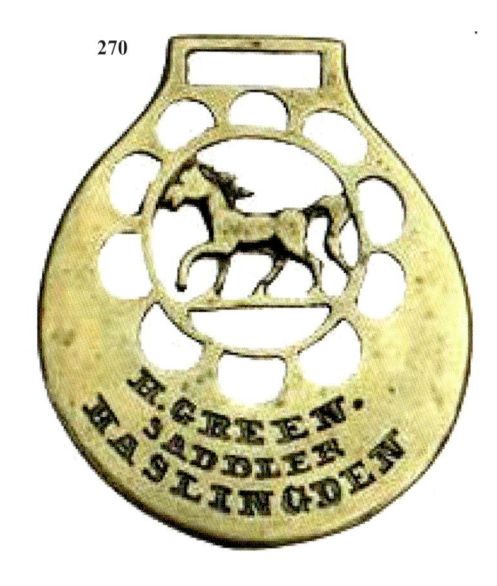

[75]

Nos. 271, 272 & 273: Frederick Curtis & Son occupied premises at 17-18 College Street in Worcester from at least 1871 to 1903 and possibly later.

No. 274: Joseph Bickerton was located at High Street West, Fenton, Stoke-on-Trent from 1874 to 1885, then at other local addresses through 1915.

No. 275: Robert Snarr Pearson of Otley, near Leeds, started in 1874 at Market Place, later moving to Westgate where he is listed from 1889 to 1907.

No. 276: Walter Mortimore had his shops on Fore Street in Cullompton and in the nearby village of Bradninch from 1874 until 1918.

No. 277: The Saddlery & Harness Stores were located at 119 Union Street in Stonehouse, Plymouth, from 1899 to 1925.

No. 278: Henry Cridland of Totnes was a maker from 1813 until the late 1850s. Like the hanging brasses on p. 32, his was one of the very earliest.

No. 279: William Henry Smith occupied premises on High Street in Bridgwater from 1880 until 1915. The business was still listed in 1933.

No. 280: William Cutts is listed from 1871 to 1896 as a saddler in Ollerton, near Mansfield, where he served the harness needs of the nearby collieries.

No. 281: Robert Williams was a saddler from 1880 until 1907 at Four Crosses, the Chwilog railway goods depot near Pwllheli in Carnarvonshire.

No. 282: John Smith is recorded at 71 Bradshaw Gate, Bolton near Manchester, from 1893 to 1903 and then at 10 Church Bank until 1940.

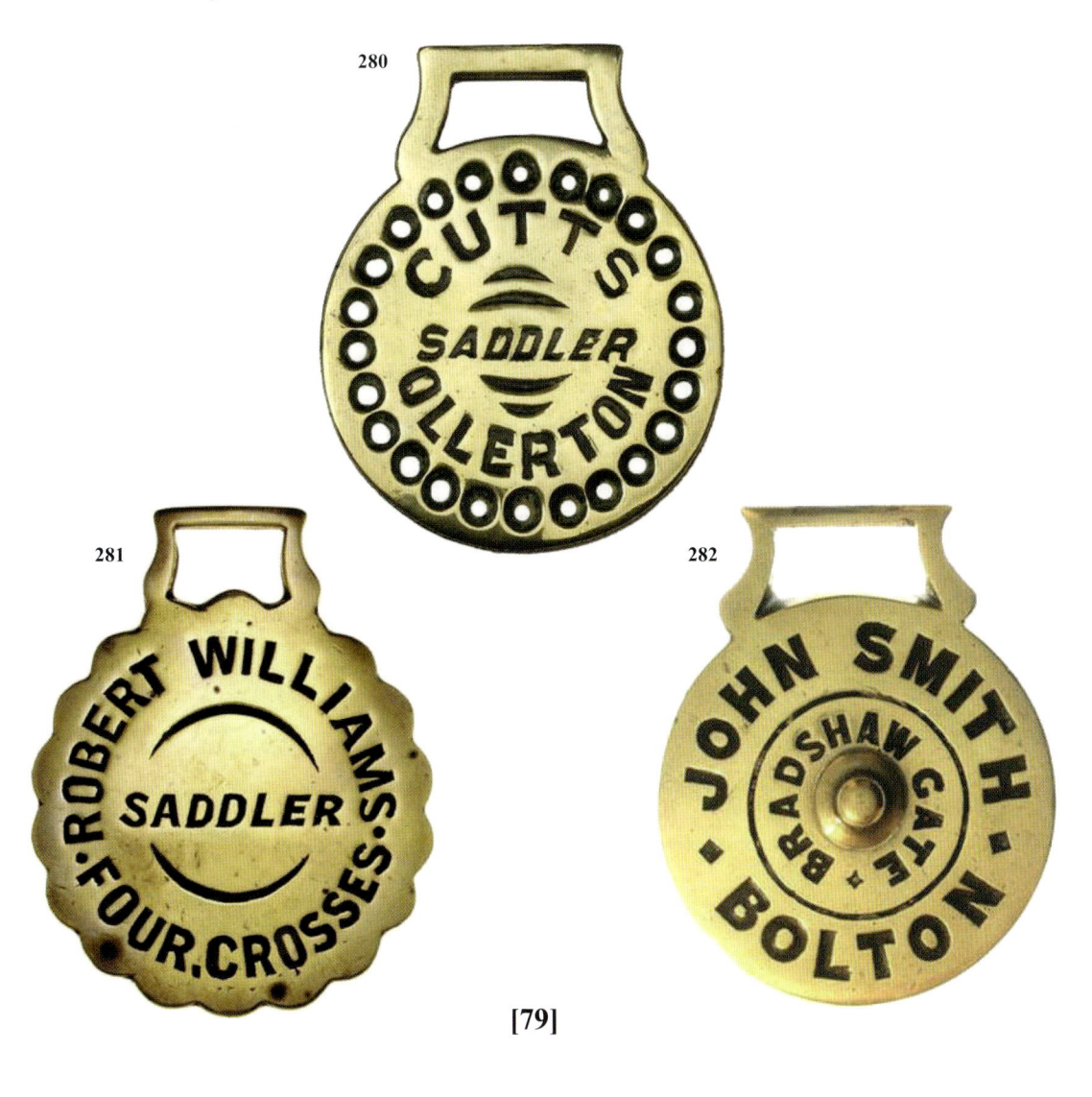

[79]

No. 283: Richard Wheatley is listed in 1880 on Salter Row at the Corn Market in Pontefract. He also had a shop on Albion Street in Castleford.

No. 284: Thomas Humphriss had shops at 65 Henley Street and 45 Wood Street in Stratford-upon-Avon from at least 1871 until 1889.

No. 285: Fred Kelk established his saddlery in 1874 on Blonk Street, Norton, at the centre of Sheffield's flourishing rail, river and canal hub. The business survived well into the 1950s, until the use of horses was finally discontinued.

No. 286:   Arthur Smith was first listed in 1893 at 19 Draper's Lane in Leominster, then from 1899 until 1937 at 18 Broad Street. His two unusual brasses were probably cast for him by Alexander and Duncan, a local foundry.

No. 287:   Henry Green of Haslingden (see example No. 270) used a different brass design to top this eye-catching advertisement for his business.

Awards

Since the publication in 1989 of Malcolm Andrews' comprehensive study, *Award Brasses*, a number of additional types have come to light from various private collections. Some may already have appeared in recent literature, but whether from local parades or ploughing matches or other events, they all enrich our perspective of an era that long ago passed into history.

288

[82]

No. 288 came from two villages in Kent, East and West Malling, which combined to form the Town Malling & District Horse Show Society. This elegant award was issued only for the years 1924-1926, during which a total of 82 were given out. Provided by Joy Bros., makers from nearby Rochester, they were presented on a leather facepiece embellished with a woollen fringe.

An annotation on the reverse of the photograph below records that "This horse and carter took 2nd Prize at the Malling Horse Show in 1927. He's also taken two or three 1st & 2nd previously for Maidstone Corporation, with driver Mr Rose [*pictured at left*]." The woollen fringed awards from preceding years may be seen hanging from the collar.

Brasses were frequently awarded at local ploughing competitions to recognise the winners. Nos. 289 and 290, issued by the Ledbury Ploughing Society in 1899 and 1900, are examples of this practice. No. 291 is a standard 1935 Jubilee brass that was adapted as a prize for the Cart Horse Parade coinciding with those celebrations in Brenchley, a village near Tonbridge in the Kent Weald. The recipient's name was engraved later.

No. 292 was awarded by the short-lived North West Essex Agricultural Association, which was organised in 1913, held two ploughing competitions in October of that year and an AGM in February 1914, then lapsed, never to revive, because of the Great War. The reverse of this prize, No. 293, is engraved to Claudius Cornell, winner in the single-furrow class at the Radwinter competition near Saffron Walden. No. 294, a similar example but only the second known to date, was presented to W.W. Symonds.

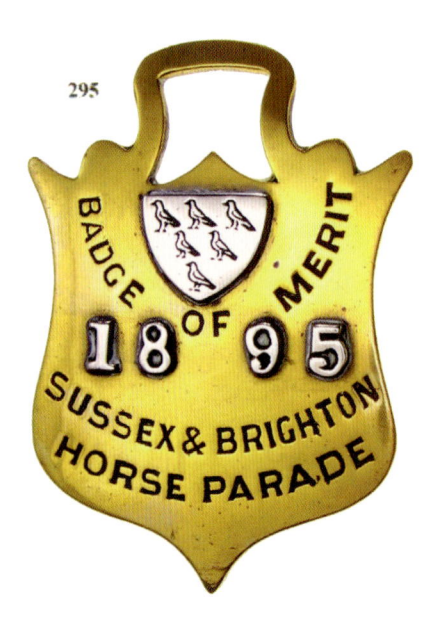

The famous Sussex & Brighton Horse Parades were held from 1893 to 1914. Example No. 295 is a merit award given in 1895. The date is displayed by individually applied white metal numerals, a unique feature found neither before nor thereafter on brasses of any type or year. In contrast, the date on No. 296 is cast intaglio, the brass itself being of a generic design that permitted its use through 1899 by secondarily adding the appropriate final digit for each year. Despite the probable issuance of many more such awards, the 1898 example shown below remains the only Sussex & Brighton Second Prize currently known to have survived. No. 297 is from Cudham, a village in Kent near Sevenoaks. The legend on this 1909 example was machine-cut.

[86]

The detailed legend engraved on example No. 298 sketches a classic local horse show in post-Edwardian rural England. It was awarded by Judge Henry Boyer to carter Bert Statten at Sonning Common near Reading in 1913.

Most of the R.S.P.C.A. London Cart Horse Parade brasses are well documented, but No. 299 was issued in 1911 with an attached royal commemorative stud, No. 299a. Could the award have been presented by King George V himself?

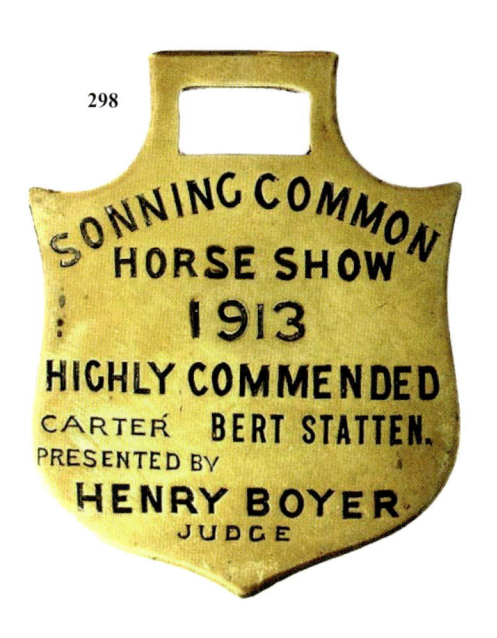

[87]

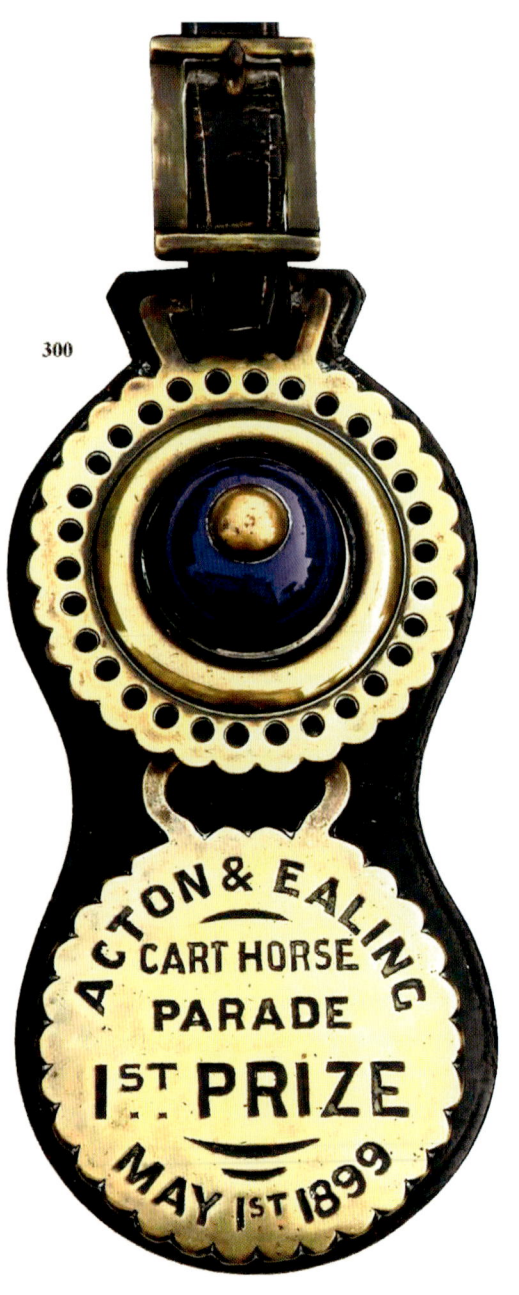

No. 300 is an intaglio-cast 1st Prize, presented at the 1899 Acton & Ealing Cart Horse Parade and still on its original shaped leather. No. 301 from the year 1890 is another such treasure, a splendid example of the first (and only) award brass ever issued by the London Carthorse Parade Society itself.

[88]

No. 302 was awarded to ploughing champion E. Carbonell in 1937 at a private competition held for employees of Chivers & Sons Ltd., owners of an 8000-acre farm near Cambridge and as famous for their magnificent Percheron horses as for their branded preserves. No. 303 is a special prize given in 1933 at the Kings Heath Horse Show near Birmingham to S.I. Reeves for "Cleanest Horse & Harness". It is worth noting that both examples utilised similar, thinly stamped brasses from contemporary stock and were presented mounted on leather, also of the period. These are important points of reference when considering the authenticity of such engraved awards.

Example No. 304 is a Merit Badge awarded at the Walsall Horse Parade in 1902. It was cast in yellow brass by Stanley Bros., a well known local foundry where the original pattern still exists. The basic design was specific to Walsall, with the date being changed each year by a separately applied capsule or ribbon. In contrast example No. 305, given as a 1st Prize in 1904, was probably less expensive to produce. It was cast in white brass and of a generic design that could be utilised by any town or group holding a horse parade on May Day of that year. Close examination shows that "Walsall" was hand-engraved at the top as a secondary operation, whereas the universal legend below had previously been cast intaglio in a different font and size.

Opposite, No. 306 features a leather-mounted stud presented to George Smith as 1st Prize for his Tradesmen's Turnout at the 1905 Enfield Horse Parade. No. 307 is another diminutive brass, a facepiece awarded at the Cheltenham Horse Parade in 1925. No. 308 was issued by the Dumb Animals Welfare Society, whose members wore a lapel badge (No. 308a, shown in actual size).

[90]

306

307

308

308a

[91]

The six brasses below and opposite, Nos. 309-314, record the impressive exploits of a race horse named "Sailor Prince" in 1887 and 1888. It is likely that the owner himself had them custom-engraved, using plain flash brasses from standard stock. The name of the successful jockey is not known.

309
Sailor Prince
CHAMPION
CUP
CAMBRIDGE
1887

310
Sailor Prince
1ST PRIZE
CAMBRIDGE
1887

311
Sailor Prince
1ST PRIZE
PETERBOROUGH
1887

[92]

[93]

Terrets

Colour and sound were important contributors to the overall spectacle of the work horse parade and therefore basic to decorated heavy harness. Multi-belled or flashing terrets adorned with flowing red, white and blue plumes were typically mounted on the cart saddle bridge of the more elaborate turnouts. The few that have survived the passage of time still evoke the pageantry and excitement of those legendary parades. Below is a prize-winning turnout from the north of England in the early 1900s, well before the invention of colour photography.

315

[95]

316

317

[97]

318

319

[99]

320

321

[101]

322

323

Oddities

Every collection has its share of mysteries, brasses of unusual design that tease the imagination but defy hard answers, those that symbolise a profession or a moment in history, and those that perhaps represent no more than pure whimsy. In closing this first volume of the *Anthology*, we offer a few of our favourites for you to ponder.

The field gate in example No. 324 might have trade significance but otherwise remains unknown. Then for facepiece No. 325, who or what does the H represent? Are the shaped cut-out and stud intended to suggest someone named Hart? Opposite, No. 326 may have been inspired by the appearance of Halley's Comet in 1910, the first time that photographs were made of this spectacular 75-year phenomenon. No. 327, the "JWT" bell, is most likely a 19th century "one-off" that belonged to John William Taylor, late owner of the famous bell foundry in Loughborough, Leicestershire. As regards cast example No. 328, was it made for some special event in 1883 or only for collectors? And did No. 329 identify a clockmaker? Finally, was No. 330 produced to commemorate the raising of Cleopatra's Needle on the Victoria Embankment in 1878?

Indeed, history guards its secrets well.

326

327

328

329

330

[105]

Acknowledgements

The authors and officers of the National Horse Brass Society wish to express their deepest gratitude for the generous support provided by members towards the production of this volume. In particular, for their kind permission to view, select, photograph and publish so many of the outstanding examples in their collections, we would like to recognise the following individuals:

Rolf Augustin, Stan Benton, Allan Brewer, Ralph Chapman, Mrs. J. Clark, Franck and Esther Desjariges, John Dew, Joe Evans, Alan Field,
Terry Keegan, Peter Lacey, Rankin Lewis, Peter Miller, Michael Mullens, Robert Prager, Mark Roberts, Stephen and Angela Standen, Keith Stevens, David Whetton, George Willett and Terry Williams.

We also pay special tribute to Michael Ferguson for his help in researching saddlers, to Rodney Jewell for use of his Strettons Derby Ales photograph, to Maurice Hill for technical advice and to Rolf Augustin for design and formatting of the book.

Thank you, one and all!

Contestants line up for a ploughing match at Diss, Norfolk, England c.1935.